More Sure

More Sure

A. Light Zachary

ARSENAL PULP PRESS
VANCOUVER

MORE SURE
Copyright © 2023 by A. Light Zachary

ARSENAL PULP PRESS
Suite 202 – 211 East Georgia St.
Vancouver, BC V6A 1Z6
Canada
arsenalpulp.com

The publisher gratefully acknowledges the support of the Canada Council for the Arts and the British Columbia Arts Council for its publishing program, and the Government of Canada, and the Government of British Columbia (through the Book Publishing Tax Credit Program), for its publishing activities.

Creation of this work was funded in part by an Ontario Arts Council grant and by a Canada Council grant.

Arsenal Pulp Press acknowledges the xʷməθkʷəy̓əm (Musqueam), Sḵwx̱wú7mesh (Squamish), and səl̓ilwətaʔɬ (Tsleil-Waututh) Nations, custodians of the traditional, ancestral, and unceded territories where our office is located. We pay respect to their histories, traditions, and continuous living cultures and commit to accountability, respectful relations, and friendship.

"In Chemicals"
Paul Murphy
© 2010 Hand Drawn Dracula
All rights reserved. Used by permission.

"Revelation #9"
Brian Warner (BMI) / Stephen Bier Jr. (BMI)
© 2007 Beat Up Your Mom Music (Admin. Dinger and Ollie Music) / Dinger and Ollie Music (c/o Songs of Mojo One)
All rights reserved. Used by permission.

Cover and text design by Jazmin Welch
Cover art and author's portrait by Saul Freedman-Lawson
Edited by John Elizabeth Stintzi
Proofread by Alison Strobel

Printed and bound in Canada

Library and Archives Canada Cataloguing in Publication:
Title: More sure : poems and interruptions / A. Light Zachary.
Names: Zachary, A. Light, author.
Identifiers: Canadiana (print) 20220412510 | Canadiana (ebook) 20220412545 |
  ISBN 9781551529172 (softcover) | ISBN 9781551529189 (EPUB)
Classification: LCC PS8649.A34 M67 2023 | DDC C811/.6—dc23

αι δεύτεραι πως φροντίδες σοφώτεραι

Εὐριπίδης

lorde i am 1 / lorde i am 2 / lorde i am infinate

Jos Charles

God particles

Hope, borne our way
in that inauspicious beak.
Hope to leave a life
in which we were taught
to deserve deuteragony.
Writing in circles
around one another
all night. Walking in circles
until, dizzy, we collide
beneath a mountain's weight
and manifest a power
that would be denied us,
were we to ask for it.
Hope and no more asking.
Let the fabric of the known
tear beyond mending.
Let it all collapse
into what we, here, comprise.
Split skies, as the world
ends, begins again:
calm on the horizon,
thunder on the wing.

Meditations, 1.

Whose soul inhabits me at this moment?
A child's, a lad's, a woman's,
a tyrant's, a dumb ox's, or a wild beast's?

Seven

When I felt as wanting for direction
as a broken, then abandoned horse,
I played the computer games
in which you could assemble people
from a bin of parts,
build their homes and plot their courses,
force them to make love or not to,
drown them when they disappoint you.
I skimmed books about emotions
for the cheat codes.
Outside the museum, after viewing dinosaurs,
I considered the wet, clumsy earth,
our shared and secret truth:
that we were both bones, all the way through.

Two girls

Somewhere, two girls are kissing for the first time
on the bathroom floor in a dark suburban basement.
They are both pretending to be boys
for one another, for themselves, for everyone
but they are two girls, kissing for the first time
on the bathroom floor in a dark suburban basement
while classmates, holding beery teenage piss,
bang on the door and urge them *hurry*.
They lift the bottom halves of their boy-masks
to free their lips, flushed pink and sparkling;
to free the soft of their liquor-wet tongues
and taste something of their truth
in the sticky roots of the other's teeth,
finding what they had not previously recognized
in their own heads, and finding it too great
to do anything with but break
into easy, dissociable pieces.
Soon, the boys they pretend to be
will get up and, through separate exits, leave the party.
The girls they really are will be left behind.
They will remain there, kissing on the floor
after the party ends and as the suburb sleeps,

after school starts up again next week
and the boys they pretend to be
pass in the hallway, silently.
They will remain there for five or ten or fifty years,
after their friend's parents' house is sold
and everybody has moved away and on with life,
after the boys have grown into pretend-men
even as they walk around empty,
having so long ago left behind their spirits:
two girls, still kissing for the first time
as shadows on the floor in a windowless room.

Palisade

Theory: epicene pronouns fit
not because I live a neuter singularity;
rather, because I contain
multitudes. Fear me.

I am coming
with a spade
across the milkweed.

I dig a hole to reach the other side of me.
I meet me in the middle.
I suppose I think alike.

And if, as I get to know myself,
I linger in the hole, it is for safety.
The hole beneath a palisade
that I and others built across my mind.

Venice

A woman I admire says I must see Venice before I die.
So that I may die at any time, I will go as soon as possible.
I will walk in circles and visit the Guggenheim museum.
I will walk backward with my eyes closed.
I will take off my clothes and swim in a canal,
shower off the dirty water and go naked on the roof.
Sit on the roof and drink wine from the Veneto,
hold myself and shiver in the wind.

The closest I have so far been to Venice
is the town of Vipiteno, deep in northern Italy.
From there, easily, I could have driven on to Venice.
But I wanted to leave something unresolved, there, in that country.
Like how I never do everything I have to do in a day
so I'll know where to start the next.
Or like how, when given a chance,
I leave a book behind in a new friend's living room
so I may see them again to collect it.
Then, if they have read it in the meantime,
we will have something to talk about.
Besides the wind, what might I talk about in Venice?

Posing for the before photo

Practise new names on baristas—see what sticks. Shoplift lipstick.
Travel freely, while you can; see Petersburg, pyramids, the heartland.
Stock your bridges with kindling, your speed-dial with hotlines—

though, really, know you will be fine
if you learn
to content yourself
with less.

After

Crash your funeral.
Wear the red dress.

Friday nights at the non-binary drive-in

A movie called *Alien vs. Predator* in which we go back in time
to fight everyone who hurt us when we were young.

A movie called *Cowboys & Aliens* about watching
our backs at the club. A movie called *Village of the Damned*

about our neighbourhood. A version of *Invasion of the
Body Snatchers* which is sympathetic to the body snatchers.

Close Encounters of the Third Kind, which is about
how we need to teach everyone we meet to communicate.

A remake of *The Island of Dr. Moreau* which portrays
the island as a medical tourism destination.

A remake of *Escape to Witch Mountain.* A movie called
[Your Name] vs. the World. A movie called *They Live.*

Palisade (outtakes)

Epicene, anthropocene, pulicene.

As B. put it: *when I say I'm bigender*
I mean I'm both the dogfucker and the dog.

I, my coyote in the doorway.
May I outdance epistemology.

The cake

Introductory questionnaire for a queer arts event, 2017

My name is: burning out of me

My pronouns are: taboo/do not speak them

                         /I will appear behind you in the mirror

My gender is: "open the oven

                 and the cake won't rise"

My sexuality is: fungal bloom on rotten wood

My disability is: shouting over distance

My past: selves, I come to matriphagic

My future: is all I have

Photo: I am fading from old photographs,

                 leaving only shadows.

                 Throw them out (and come take new ones/

                      I'll be on stage tonight)

Someday You'll Love _____ Zachary

I spend a year soft-launching my reintroduction, trying to say: *I am kind of between names, these days,* and then I give up trying, the people cannot fucking take it,

can you imagine Adam's outrage had some beast refused the name he gave it, the people with their language and their pitiable need to feel secure in its dominion

over me (*What should I call you?* Never call me), agency in language is invalid when you claim it for yourself, apparently, I walk into the party and they hail me:

The Artist Formerly Known as ████, as if that isn't still an invocation, I should have got a D.N.R. tattoo before I shed that skin,

the people and their brittle ways of knowing, how they seek to shut me in, they plead with me, but I am become fugitive, picker of locks (behind every door, I find the rest of me).

Qubit

The engineer, my father, is perfecting
his second quantum computer. I was the first;
bigender life is superposition, basically.
Wigner's girlfriend. Schrödinger's coyote.

His dream has been to wield Alexander's sword
against knots of encryption so complex,
they have never yet been tied, even in theory.
He failed, with me. I do the opposite,
creating such tangles in our conversations daily.

In his laboratory, I am introduced: his *son*.
Light, squeezed. Into something he can see.
My newborn sister can fit inside his palm.
She might achieve in seconds
what would take me immortality.

Cratylus, 1.

*I can conceive no correctness of names other than this;
you give one name, and I another.*

Cratylus, 2.

Suppose that I call a [faggot] *a* [dyke] *or a* [dyke] *a* [faggot], *you mean to say that a* [faggot] *will be rightly called a* [dyke] *by me individually, and rightly called a* [faggot] *by the rest of the world; and a* [dyke] *again would be rightly called a* [faggot] *by me and a* [dyke] *by the world:—that is your meaning?*

All ten parts

Eventually, we might take it to the streets like Elagabalus, resplendent. We might take it to the seas, like the clownfish—that clutch of sunset in the deep—who, when deigning to breed, switches sex to domme the prettiest boy in the anemone (he should be so lucky). But, for now, let non-binary supremacy begin at home, in bed. For all our oppressors may keep from our reach, they will never know what it is to ████████ so decadently as we do. They already hate us for this freedom they can't eat; they might slay us all if they knew how ██████ it can be to embody confluence, incarnate possibility. Come, take it to the kitchens with me: trans sex is adding to your mother's recipe until it's your recipe—tripling the heat, substituting meat for flowers. Straight men tell me that nothing arouses like the new, and we can know that satisfaction every time. Come, sit on my face until you change its shape; let us make belief from what we were told was waste. *Disinfect me, resurrect me.* Let a revolution spark in the negative space between a boy's cunt and seven inches of clitoris. Let two photons meet. Let us spurn wolves in woke clothing— let us t4t. All we need is another who knows to see and be seen by the unseen; to hold and be held, adore and be adored, to believe and be believed by the word, before the body.

Definit

Be born.

So as to give a specified impression.

Switch on.

Begin to burn; be ignited.

Drunk.

A blank space to be filled by a letter.

Spiritual illumination by divine truth.

To suddenly become animated with liveliness or joy.

Fluffy and well aerated during cooking.

An indication that a long period of difficulty is nearing an end.

Someday I'll Love _____ Zachary

Someday, I'll love myself by whatever my name will be.
I will introduce myself so effortlessly;
come when called in the café or doctor's office,
invite the eyes of strangers to affix it to me.
I have been seeking it in dictionaries, poetry,
in my view of trees, the sky, the city—call me
all of that. Wind in leaves, gum stuck to the street—
call me something ubiquitous, genderless, and sweet.
As part of me as a hand that I hold out to shake,
inseparable as the nail and its bed beneath;
someday, a name as no hand-me-down has fit me
by which I might love myself. I'll sing it, constantly;
a rhythm that'll build, spill out of me, revealing it
to all, and I'll be ready. You will know me by its certainty.

Satires, 1.

Who will guard [me from] *the guards?*

Satires, 2.

Even those who don't want to kill [me] want the power to do it.

Satires, 3.

The fantastic size of [my] *cock will get* [me] *precisely nowhere.*

Satires, 4.

Pray for a sound mind in [another] *body.*

Satires, 1. (remix)

Who will police the policemen who tear the sundress from my lover, aged fourteen, and throw her nude to the holding cell floor? Who will sue the suits who voted for their right to delete the footage from the cameras in the room? Who will set her parents to their duties as she cleans her wounds alone? As she is made to feel she is a wound? Who will cure her of what doctors refuse to do, or educate teachers who refuse to teach her? Who will correct those who believe their abuse to be corrective, protect her from those who mask hatred in claims that they seek to protect her? Who will right the self-righteous? Who will judge the judges, or advocate against the devil's advocates? The guards are coming— who will guard her?

Not travelling

We are looking at panoramic images on Google Maps
of high-resolution beauty in lands we will never visit
because we would have to wear disguises there
and we are too proud for that.
Panoramic images of fertile plains
where the people like us, buried in hasty graves,
get dug up by starving dogs.
Valleys where the people like us are starving dogs.
Panoramic images of cities where the sun does
dazzling things to the tiles on the walls,
where our unmet siblings' blood
trickles out from alleys.
No images are uploaded from inside the alleys.
Panoramic images with the faces blurred out.

Bye

Poet, do you really love the moon,
or do you love what the moon represents to you?
I know of a poet's need to use things.
People, too. A poet used a rock
when he thought: *I will build a church upon it.*
Any rock would have done, really.
Flesh or celestial, any body
that would have revolved around you
as you worked out your frustration.
Tidally bound to face your idealization,
the moon only has that dark side because of you—
because of what you are, not what you lack.
Poet, you know your orbit is a trap;
how can you pretend it stays because it loves you back?

Feedback loop

~~Fuck me so good, we can forget what gender is and how it burdens us. So good, we forget we have been known by others by names other than the names we call each other when alone, or mostly. Fuck me so it's just us two and our phones on silent, just me and a dream of reversed polarity, in the rush to come before dysphoria derails this again. Early morning, before daylight can get in and bring with it reality.~~ *~~I would do anything to know how this feels for you,~~* ~~either one of us could say — and we both are thinking — but instead, we keep up the feedback loop of endearments we have longed to hear, may not otherwise receive. You call me your woman so sweetly, I can almost believe it. I call you~~ *~~mine,~~* ~~you imagine how it might feel to belong. This proves too much for you — you bite my shoulder to stifle the pitch of your cry. Later, you cry against the bruise in the shower after sunrise, stripped of the lies that got us through~~

Dog person

Sunlight bends around corners, winds its way into your eyes too early, you're tired, always tired, you love me but lament my paper blinds, you love somebody else, he who lives three time zones to the west, and you prefer to stay up late making him come over the phone, bullying it out of him, that's what he likes, sending pictures of your tongue, pictures of my blanket draped around your shoulders, you love me but don't let me make you breakfast, you're never hungry in the morning, always sick on little sleep and vinho verde, you two love to drink together, I drop off in pauses in the laughter from the other room, we share a bed, when I wake I try to hold you, coax you with kisses in your hair, but you push me back, still dreaming, mumbling something about a cat, I'm allergic and you rue that, I know you wish we could have a cat, *a little bastard*, but I'm glad we can't, I couldn't take more of that energy, I'm a dog person, need to feel a little like you couldn't go without me, I can't sit around all day just hoping I might get to pet you, I mean, the sun's been up for hours, now, and I'm still playing ukulele quiet in the bathroom, any polyamorous love song hides notes of resentment in its tune, like Bach signed his name, like Marilyn Manson and his backmasked messages, such as, *once you've been here, brothers and sisters; there ain't no going back. You are on the other side now. There ain't no going back*

Poem (after Matthew Rohrer)

You called, you're on the train, on Sunday.
Who built that railway on a coin's edge,
anyhow. Who packed your bags, I helped.
I peeled and sliced an apple. By the time
you find the Ziploc of fetid, pulpy evidence
in your duffle pocket, it will emit a quiet heat.
You taught me to compost, once: to spread
my old ideas over planted fields, pray for green.
But you took the seeds. You called to say that
you took the seeds, you needed them, you're sorry.

Palisade (coyote version)

And as in *I am*.
I live as in *despite*.

I dig a hole.
I have no choice.

Both sides—
where will I sleep tonight?

Why bury yourself in this place you ask

Sonnets on the salt marsh, clearing hurricane debris

She would never put my sister to this work,
but part of coming home is being what she needs,
and a second daughter
isn't it.

                                    How many
                  of those who came before me

                            lived as men, simply
              because there was too much to do?

           Who thought, whatever I am, this is the form it takes;
                                 put it to use.

When I'm away, she lives alone, give or take some crows.
She feeds them. In return, asks only
that they come each morning to be fed.
(*If I'm dead, they'll be the first to know.*) It was once so easy.

Once upon a broken, shingle-stripped shed roof—

Once upon a woodpile soaked through, tripled in weight—

Once upon a porcupine's skull crushed beneath a boot—

Once upon a shallow dune, ruptured by the waves—

Once upon a daughter-son in stinking, sinking dirt—

Once upon a jellyfish, wind-beaten into gum—

Once upon a biting fly that finds an eyelet in my shirt—

Once upon a rusty nail, once upon a thumb—

Once upon a painted nail, once upon a callused hand—

Once upon the shadow I project across the haul—

Once upon an oyster float half-buried in the sand—

Once upon a tidal flat, pressed flatter every fall—

Once upon, from the house beyond, a mother's gaze—

I perform what is expected of me, and am praised.

Not that I really mind. It's honest work.
Shaking the sweat from my hair like a dog
as I push the wheelbarrow home.
From outside the kitchen window,
I watch the women talk, but I can't hear them.
My mother thanks me when I get inside.
Her sister fetches me a beer and says,
il est plus tough qu'il n'y paraît, non?
How else to take that but as a compliment?
Still, as I pass, she grabs my skinny arm
and my hackles raise. Whatever. I'm too tired
to do anything but slip upstairs to hide, where I
won't risk saying something I'll regret; after all,
there's work to be done about my honesty.

There's work to be done about my honesty.
There's an earnestness that I can't shake.
It's a well-built, steady home;
no sound travels through the windows.
I watch the women talk, but I can't hear them.
They change the subject when I get inside.
I'll never know what they say about me,
how I seem to them. Still, my other side—
the favourite son—can take their compliments,
pass them up to my mother like ribbons
to hang on the fridge. Whatever I am,
whatever of me I may need to hide,
I know I would regret depriving her of this—
not that I really mind. It's honest work.

x-large rubber-ringed
wheel of the barrow kicks up
red salt mud as I
lose my footing stumble back
a crack beneath a boot heel

She never talked about [he who would have been] my brother until I was twenty. She didn't need to; it had always felt clear that I held too much to be a firstborn son. My first step was in his shadow.

my next careless step
pulverizes porcupine's
skull a second time

Sometimes, when I comfort my mother, set her at ease with the half of me she knows—the only half she needs—I see that shadow in the room. It flickers on the floor between us, in a shape like might have been his;

broader at the shoulders, nearly as tall as me. Which of us calls it here?
Who needs him more?

> scraps of mottled hair
> cling around its empty eyes
> stuck with browning blood

I don't see his shadow on the salt marsh, in the sweeping calligraphy of the
wind in its grass. It's overcast—hurricane aftermath. (Dorian, after a boy
who never aged.) But in my mind's eye, I conjure him forth and give him
strong hands (*il est plus tough*) which work alongside mine. He offers to
yank the oyster cage from the muck, or drag the heavy driftwood home;
offers me the option to be weak.

> scraped up on the spade
> slipped into the knotted brush
> rest and be forgotten

plastic fence

buoy

lumber

~~me~~ firewood

jellyfish (dead)

oyster float

oysters (dead?)

firewood

too wet to burn

~~firewood~~

rotting wood

or to build with

~~lumber~~ rot

rot

The x-large, rubber-ringed wheel of the barrow
kicks up red salt mud as I lose my footing,
ram the fucking thing into the only rock in sight.
Next week in the city, I'll wear the same jeans
on stage, stains and all, to perform a saccharine
poem on my pussy; meanwhile, scarlet flecks
now chipping off my nails will float on the tide.
Both sides, but ever leaving detritus behind,
carrying mementoes of my other home with me.
What does it mean to be a man on clay
and a woman on concrete? To trip between the two?
Quick-change wizard of the WestJet washroom,
I emerge with a new face, another name—
and, yet, a sheen of suspect residue.

Red oak

In the abyss of instinct
between my ideology
and the scent I pull from the air
when you raise your arms
to lift your sister's child
(it's summer, your season
and the windows of your sleeves
are open wide)
I register new distance
between the limitations
of the form
and what I would express.
You teach
and she recites
Linnaean names of trees;
you swell with pride.
You tell her, *take a leaf*
from the highest branch
you help her reach
for proof of where she's been
and in my belly,
I can feel the gnarled stub

of what could have been the fist
I could have clenched you in.
If my gut swells with anything,
it's garbage.
If my breasts were to swell
they'd swell with polysiloxanes
synthesized from plastics
which, in turn, are synthesized
from the bottomless decay
that underscores the world I know.
Another ankle twisted
in the rabbit hole.
Suddenly, the girl has to pee.
You swing her down. She meets
the grass with tiny Nikes—
third-grade fresh,
new and white as her own teeth.
She runs back to the house
and you watch her go
with a look on your face like
you're watching your future
run towards you.
I hope your future is out there,
running towards you.
I wouldn't know.
I'm just sitting here
with a look on my face like

I'm watching a garden on fire.
Who would plant a garden
in the abyss between
your street
and my most bromidic fantasy?
(How selflessly
you would have loved our child,
how selfishly our child
would have loved this world.
The cool-rock collection
at their bedside,
how it would have sparkled
in the dawn.)
You are the only thing
I can't accept about my body,
the only door
actually closed to me.
Next week,
I'll try to run the other way—
spare you any more
of this bitterness
and leave:
So that I might
yet drain the venom
from this inveterate wound,
spit it down the sink,
fix my lipstick, and be free.

Transgender Dysphoria Blues

Walking in the valley of the shadow
with my headphones on. And learning to put
the *cunt in* my *strut*
to the break of her song.

For women who look too closely

~~Yes: I shave, I tweeze. I slather primer (×2), C.C. cream,~~
~~concealer. I conceal. Lay foundation~~
~~so that I might build a house of femininity upon my face.~~
~~I paint the shutters blue. I blink the dust away.~~
~~This is no steady ground; every night, the house~~
~~collapses. I'm not bothered. I sleep~~
~~rough. Beneath the leaves. I wake. I shave, I tweeze~~—You want the poem of me plucking hairs from bleeding cheeks while I weep at the futility, but I cannot understand it as futility; every time I build a house, I build it better. You want the poem of me clawing at the dirt beneath my eyes as if burrowing a den in which to hide, but upon this plot, I write the poem in which, hammer over highlighter, I construct a higher zygomatic arch. The poem dancing through. I write the poem about your fear of what it means that something like me can be better at this than you.

Hercules

'Tis the first art of [queens], *the power to suffer hate.*

Bumper sticker

MY OTHER [gender] *IS A FERRARI*

Thirteen

Still awake on itchy carpet.
Still, he sleeps between
sheets textured by the grit
he tracks in. I had to
leave, but didn't feel I had
the leave to go too far.
Plus, I might be bleeding?
I failed to prepare.
Next time, I'll do better.
He believes in me.
That's what he tells me.
I wonder whether I will
glow in the morning.
Like women say they do.
Whether he will want me
once I glow. Or if only
dullness draws him.
Why he calls me *kid*
and still he fucked me.
How he reconciles this.
What the logic points to.
Whether he will want me

once the seed
he planted in me
sprouts. Spoiler: no.
Men will promise things.
He's about to teach me this.
He has never taught me
anything, and I'm excited.
Dawn becomes him—
backlights his profile
as if in eclipse.
Still, he sleeps between
me and the sun, between
me and the window.
There is no door to enter
or to leave the room.

Hi

It's me, the coyote, again.
In an evening gown.

Pretty, painted claws
and all

but still rooting
through your garbage.

My field

Shattered glass in rug
enacts a minefield.
Fabric pills with blood
as you crawl into the valley
of what it is to love
one breaking on the question:
if to err is human,
what is mine.
My field and I
in all my glory.
The temples
rupturing around me.
Still, your augury;
you claim to see a future
where I only see foam
on the lips of steeds.
Still, you endure me
only to cover me
up in all my glory,
interrupt me
with the tender press
of one red, tearing knee.

Archivists

It lives in *I love you* as it lives in *I'm scared, too.*
It lives in *be careful*, it lives in *welcome home.*
It lives in every late-night subway ride survived alone,
these days, as it lives in every risk we hesitate

to let each other take. It lives in our never throwing
old tickets, little notes, or anything at all away—
every twinned scrap an artifact, our pockets shrines.
Your wallet bulges with what-if-it-were-to-happen
as my closet fills with this-would-be-all-I'd-have;
my handwritten lines, your sweaty shirts in sealed bags.

It lives in, while you stir from sleep around me,
my lifting high the camera to immortalize this deeply
mortal thing. Look at how it lives in this one:
safe, for now, and tangled in this shroud of dawn,

how it is alive.   *Good morning—is it raining?*

Meditations, 2.

At first light have in readiness, against disinclination to leave your bed, the
thought that "I am rising for the work of [becoming]

[examining]

[mirroring]

[overcoming]

[repenting]

[transcending]

[unbecoming] [wo/]*man"*.

Community

You who live in daytime,
do not disparage us
for our reluctance
to leave our fire's light.

Overwrite

Do not kiss, but bite apart the scar.
Let it heal anew—

like a bone that must be broken worse
to grow back right;

unlike how I decide to make the best of this life,
rather than reset and try again.

Give me the power to allow you power over me.
The power to allow you, or anyone, back in.

Feedback loop (remix)

Stripping you of the lies that get you through this life; speaking you free of any name that came before the one you're trying on this week; pulling you out from underneath ideas of gender that would seek to keep you still; pulling you out long and slowly, taking my time, derailing any hope dysphoria might have of slipping in around the sides of your blindfold with the sunrise. Sunrise. Following its gold across your skin—or is that not the sunrise. Falling into you, into this feedback loop of feeling, its current crackling and sparking green at every place we meet. We call each other *mine*, sink our teeth into the other's neck to prove it, stifling the triumph in our cries while our parents sleep below. I fall into you until I can fall no higher; fall, for you to pick me up again. *I would do anything,* I begin—but I leave it there. You know.

The conservator

Will I find equal beauty
in freshening this tired face
once more?
In replacing what each humid summer
took as toll,
sealing cracks,
preserving the idea of a whole
and then retreating,
leaving no trace to gaze untrained
of the work I've done
to keep the atmosphere at bay—
will I find beauty equal
to that I could find
in stripping it away?
There is a temptation
to the canvas' forgotten grain.
There are no end of sayings
re. the inspiration
to be found
in the unspoiled page.
Still, when temptation strikes,
I think of the girl in France

who poisoned the sea of white

(a Twombly)

with a lipstick kiss;

how I want to leave no room

for anyone to come upon this

work and see a thing

to try and make their own,

to stain.

I would rather frame, reframe,

overfill its holes

until but a stroke

of the original remains,

than allow it

to suffer the vulnerability

in what it would mean

to begin again.

Animula (after Hadrian)

Little soul. Vagabond.
What else? What now?
What side of town
will you end up on?
Naked, blue, and frozen
into place. With—at last—
that puppy smile
missing from your face.

To recite each morning

Know myself.
Let grow myself.

Unmask myself.
Unman myself.

Unname myself.
Unchain myself.

Undefine myself.
Unexplain myself.

Unjustify myself.
Unrationalize myself.

Unpatient myself.
Unkind myself.

Unstation myself.
Unroot myself.

Unsettle myself.
Unsuit myself.

Unwall myself.
Unroof myself.

Unstall myself.
Unleash myself.

Free myself.

Free myself.

Free myself.

The coyote speaks

Deliberate
    is life
        in the city.
        We learn
        and lapse
        in language,
        stain our coat
        to match
        the shade
        in alleys.
        We make
        a dance
        of dodging
        cars,
        weave
        as needles
        through
        our secret ways.
        We sharpen
        our ears
        on every stone
        thrown,

grow
in readying
for every fight
we face.
Men call us
different names.
They hate us.
They fear
we might take
their sons.
To eat,
or to make
them wild, too.
(Which
the viler fate.)
Still,
it is no miracle
that we
have lived
this long.
Deliberate
is life
in the refusal
to starve,
the refusal
to be preyed
upon.

We look

into windows,

ask:

what luxury

is stasis,

really.

They who never

change,

what can they

know

for sure.

What can they

learn about

shelter

if they never

sleep beneath

the stars.

What can they

learn about

the stars

if the stars

are ever

in their favour.

How will they

know their way

home

if they never

have to

leave.

How will they

know

this is where

they're meant

to be.

Who are they,

really.

And who

told them

that.

What are they

living in

response to.

As we rise

to meet

a city

where, once,

a cage

was built

around us

as we lay asleep.

A city

that would

see us

fall behind.

Deliberate

is life

in our refusal

to.

Let us now

take pride

in our refusal.

Who could know

becoming

as we do.

The power in

what it is

to live with such

intention—   (sing it

with me:) *we become*

more sure

of who we are

than you.

Toronto, Grande-Digue, Banff, New York, Venice.
2015 to 2022.

notes

by page

9.   The first epigraph is from Euripides' *Hippolytos*. Translators tend to interpret this line as: *Second thoughts are always wiser*. Upon this and related passages, classicist Emily McDermott writes: "When [Euripides] placed himself in the extraordinary position of presenting on the Athenian stage a 're-production' of his original *Hippolytos*, that was a situation he could not let pass in silence. He therefore conceptualized his modifications in plot and characterization as a change of mind, and at several key points during the play invested characters' words with a double meaning reflective of the authorial 'second thoughts' by which he had revamped his plot."

9.   The second epigraph is from Jos Charles' *feeld*.

15.   "*Meditations, 1.*" is a repurposed quotation from Marcus Aurelius' *Meditations* (trans. Staniforth).

24.   "Palisade (outtakes)" paraphrases a line from Jean Valentine's poem "Coyote."

29.   "Qubit" liberally borrows from the lexicon of quantum mechanics. *Light, squeezed* refers to "squeezed states of light"—nonclassical states of light whose noise levels, at certain phases, may fall below that of the vacuum state (i.e., of no light at all). Created in non-linear

optical interactions, these states reduce quantum uncertainty in a photonics-based quantum computing system. Also, my name is Light. It's a pun. You're welcome.

30, 31. "*Cratylus,* 1." and "2." are repurposed and interrupted quotations, respectively, from Plato's *Cratylus* (trans. Jowett).

32. "All ten parts" finds its title in the tale of Tiresias, especially as recorded in the *Bibliotheca* of Pseudo-Apollodorus. An oft-invoked Theban prophet, Tiresias was born a man, but spent seven years transformed into a woman as punishment for offending Hera. Later in his life, when asked by Zeus and Hera whether sexual intercourse—in Tiresias' experience—was better enjoyed by women or men, he replied: *if the pleasures of love be reckoned at ten, men enjoy one and women nine* (trans. Frazer). Upon hearing this, Hera burned out his eyes for unclear reasons. The poem also includes a lyric from "In Chemicals," as written and performed by Postdata.

33. "Definit" uses ten of the *Oxford English Dictionary*'s 57 definitions for *light*.

37–40. "*Satires,* 1." through "4." interrupt quotations from Juvenal's *Satires* (trans. Ramsay).

45. "Dog person" recalls the title of Jacob Wren's *Polyamorous Love Song* and includes lyrics from "Revelation #9," as written and performed by Marilyn Manson.

46. "Poem (after Matthew Rohrer)" was written after Matthew Rohrer's "Poem," and shares its first line.

51. "Why bury yourself in this place you ask" uses a line from Douglas Lochhead's *High Marsh Road* as its title.

63. "Red oak" shares an image with Julian Talamantez Brolaski's poem "against breeding."

66. *"Transgender Dysphoria Blues"* is a response to the album of the same name, written by Laura Jane Grace and performed by Against Me!

68. *"Hercules"* interrupts a line from Seneca's *Hercules* (trans. Miller).

77. *"Meditations, 2."* interrupts a line from Marcus Aurelius' *Meditations* (trans. Staniforth).

80. "Feedback loop (remix)" draws from at least one of Phyllis Webb's *Naked Poems*.

83. "Animula (after Hadrian)" is a loose translation based on a deliberate misreading of Hadrian's poem "Animula Vagula Blandula," often known in English as "Little Soul."

acknowledgments

I am grateful for the support and hospitality of the Banff Centre for Arts and Creativity, where I completed the first draft of this book. I am grateful for the support of the Canada Council for the Arts, Ontario Arts Council, Lambda Literary Foundation, and Access Copyright Foundation.

Some of these poems were first published in *Arc Poetry Magazine*, cv2, *Foglifter*, *The Malahat Review*, *Plenitude*, *Poetry Is Dead*, prism international, *Room*, *The Rumpus*, and *Witch Craft*, and in *Emerge*, an anthology published by the Lambda Literary Foundation in 2021.

"Two girls" and "Why bury yourself in this place you ask" were separately nominated for the cbc Poetry Prize in 2021.

Thanks to my teachers: Dionne Brand, Kevin Connolly, and A.F. Moritz.

Thanks to ten generous early readers: Samuel Ace, Eduardo C. Corral, Saul Freedman-Lawson, Jack Hawk, Aisha Sasha John, Daniel Sarah Karasik, F.A. Meier, Noor Naga, Karen Solie, and Kai Cheng Thom. Thanks also to Jo Ianni, the very first fan of my work.

John Elizabeth Stintzi: if I am one parent of this book, you're the other.

Thanks to my supportive and patient parents. Thanks to my dear friend, Alexander. Thanks, again, to Jack, for and despite everything.

A. Light Zachary is a writer, editor, artist, and an autistic, queer human who lives between Tkaronto (Toronto) and Signigtewa'gi (New Brunswick), Canada. *More Sure* is their first book of poems.

alightzachary.com   @alightupon